A to Z finding a pet for me

By: Merav Ben Oved

Editing: Kay Derochie
Cover design: Reut Haver, Osher studio

©2017 by Merav Ben oved

All rights reserved. No part of this publication may be reproduced, distributed, or transmitted in any form or by any means, including photocopying, recording, or other electronic or mechanical methods, without prior written permission of the author, except in case of brief quotations embodied in critical reviews and certain other noncommercial uses permitted by copyright law.

Dedicated with all my love to the light of my life, my beautiful daughter, Yuli Ben Oved, who has been the inspiration for this book and an active participant in its creation.

I have been looking for the perfect pet.
So my friend said, "Go to our local vet."
His office was filled from A to Z.
All wanted their favorite pet for me.

What a contest!

Letter A argued I should take an ant.
She's climbing up an asparagus plant.
See her running around all summer long,
Saving food for winter, so she'll be strong.

My, oh my, it is so unclear.
Is this my perfect pet I hear?
The ant is amusing but how can I know?
There are so many letters with pets to show.

Did you know?
Ant societies have division of labor, communication between individuals, and an ability to solve complex problems.

Letter B believed I should get a bear,
A real buddy, covered in brown hair.
The busy bee gave him a bad scare,
But he was so brave, he did not care.

My, oh my, it is so unclear.
Is this my perfect pet I hear?
The bear's beautiful, but how can I know?
There are so many letters with pets to show.

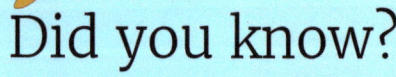

Did you know?

Most bears move into dens for a long winter sleep. They can go for more than 100 days without eating, drinking, urinating, or defecating.

Letter C cried, "Consider a cat.
This cute little pet can sure scare a rat.
Clean and fluffy, he is clearly cuddly.
On cold nights, he warms you up doubly."

My, oh my, it is so unclear.
Is this my perfect pet I hear?
The cat is courageous, but how can I know?
There are so many letters with pets to show.

Did you know?
One third of cats' awake time is usually spent cleaning themselves.

Letter D declared, "Get a decent dog,
And go together for a daily jog!
A loyal friend, you'll definitely keep,
Even if he gets dirty digging deep."

My, oh my, it is so unclear.
Is this my perfect pet I hear?
A dog is delightful, but how can I know?
There are so many letters with pets to show.

Did you know?
Dogs have a sixth sense: they are sensitive to the earth's magnetic field.

E entered with a huge elephant.
Two big ears, he looked so elegant.
"His long, long trunk will get you soaking wet,
The funniest pet you could ever get."

My, oh my, it is so unclear.
Is this my perfect pet I hear?
Elephants are exciting, but how can I know?
There are so many letters with pets to show.

Did you know?
Male African elephants are the world's largest land animals now living. They can reach a height of 13 ft. (4 m.) and weigh 15,000 lb (7,000 kg).

F figured a fat frog would be fun,
Jumping freely and playing in the sun.
A princess's kiss might make him prince
For them to live happily ever since.

My, oh my, it is so unclear.
Is this my perfect pet I hear?
A frog is fantastic, but how can I know?
There are so many letters with pets to show.

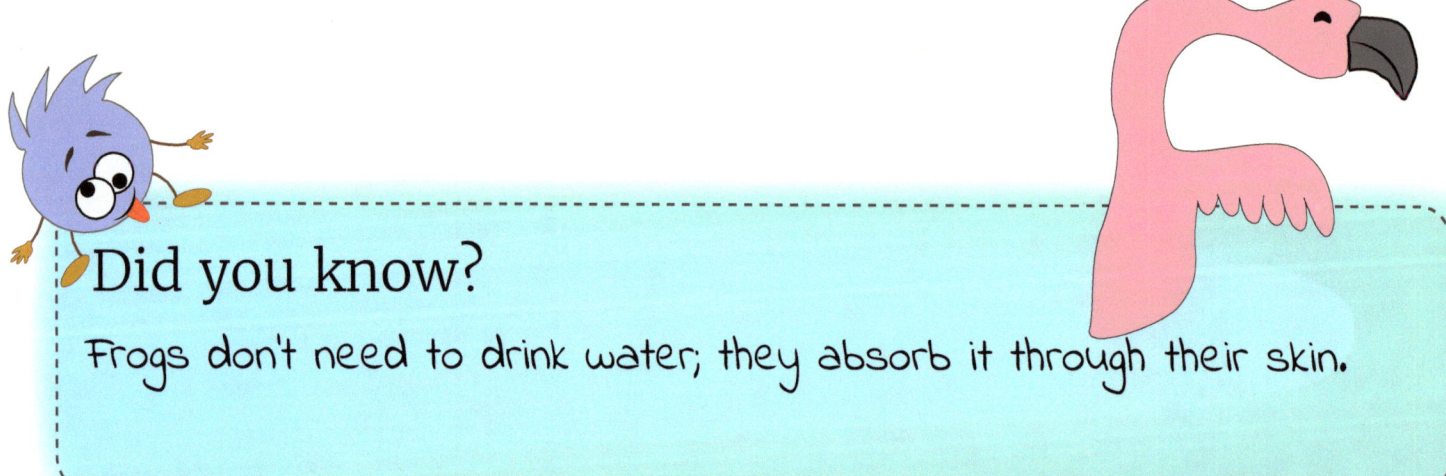

Did you know?
Frogs don't need to drink water; they absorb it through their skin.

G gave me a young gorilla, all black.
He'll mature into a great silverback.
A giant, but gentle and really shy,
He likes fruits and veggies, wouldn't hurt a fly.

My, oh my, it is so unclear.
Is this my perfect pet I hear?
Gorillas are gorgeous, but how can I know?
There are so many letters with pets to show.

Did you know?

Gorillas will groom each other by combing each other with their fingers and teeth.

H hurried in, high on his noble horse,
"Sure to make you hugely happy, of course.
Riding on his back, you will have a blast.
Then, hopefully, he will get you home fast."

My, oh my, it is so unclear.
Is this my perfect pet I hear?
The horse is heroic, but how can I know?
There are so many letters with pets to show.

Did you know?

Horses can sleep both lying down and standing up. Horses will stand together head to tail and use their tails to keep flies off the other horse's head.

I thought an iguana was ideal.
"He sure can identify a good meal.
A third eye on his head, spines on his back.
He'll play dead while enjoyment you'll not lack."

My, oh my, it is so unclear.
Is this my perfect pet I hear?
Iguanas are in; but how can I know?
There are so many letters with pets to show.

Did you know?
Iguanas can change their color. Their skin works as a camouflage, allowing them to blend with the landscape.

J held a jellyfish in a huge jar.
I jumped to set it free, not too far,
Free to swim joyfully in the big sea.
Just be careful of his sting, that's the key.

My, oh my, it is so unclear.
Is this my perfect pet I hear?
A jellyfish! You're joking for all I know.
I'll wait for other letters with pets to show.

Did you know?
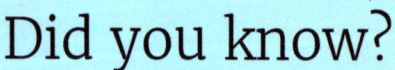
If a jellyfish is cut in two, the pieces can grow two new jellyfish.

K was so keen on a kangaroo mom.
A baby in her pouch, she keeps him calm.
Her tail is muscular, her head is small.
With two large legs, she jumps over the wall.

My, oh my, it is so unclear.
Is this my perfect pet I hear?
Kangaroos are kinda cool, but how can I know?
There are so many letters with pets to show.

Did you know?
Kangaroos can jump three times their own height.

L liked lion, his roar loud and clear
Likely to fill your enemies with fear.
His luxurious mane is very long.
King of animals, he's lethally strong!

My, oh my, it is so unclear.
Is this my perfect pet I hear?
The lion is lovely, but how can I know?
There are so many letters with pets to show.

Did you know?

In the wild, lions rest for around 20 hours a day. When a lion wakes up and roars, it can be heard from 5 miles (8 kilometers) away.

M marched in with a silly monkey.
He mimics people and is so spunky.
He's madly curious and mostly smart,
Hiding a mango in the market cart.

My, oh my, it is so unclear.
Is this my perfect pet I hear?
Monkeys are marvelous, but how can I know?
There are so many letters with pets to show.

Did you know?

Monkeys use different pitches to warn of danger, call a mate, or communicate with their young.

N noted, "Get a nightingale singer.
Even at night, he will never linger,
Migrating to Africa (what a quest!),
Returning in spring to his comfy nest."

My, oh my, it is so unclear.
Is this my perfect pet I hear?
A nightingale is neat, but how can I know?
There are so many letters with pets to show.

Did you know?
It's only the male nightingale that sings. He sings to attract a mate.

O offered an octopus in motion,
Jetting fast through the wide-open ocean,
Eight long legs and one quite odd-looking beak.
He'll occasionally fish and crabs seek.

My, oh my, it is so unclear.
Is this my perfect pet I hear?
An octopus is okay, but how can I know?
There are so many letters with pets to show.

Did you know?
An octopus can grow a lost arm. Scientists are studying this ability to learn about how we people might possibly be able to grow new tissue when we are injured.

P promised me a panda; she's so sweet,
Pretty with her black patches and white feet.
Giant bamboo is her favorite food,
Perfect for getting her in a good mood.

My, oh my, it is so unclear.
Is this my perfect pet I hear?
A panda is precious but how can I know?
There are so many letters with pets to show.

Did you know?

Pandas feed almost entirely on bamboo. Bamboo is so nutritionally poor that pandas have to eat up to 44 lb (20 kg) each day, which can take up to 16 hours.

Q quickly quacked in with a quirky quail.
Quite full of brown spots, she is never pale.
"Small speckled eggs she quietly lays,
One egg at a time for each of your days."

My, oh my, it is so unclear.
Is this my perfect pet I hear?
A quail could qualify, but how can I know?
There are still more letters with pets to show.

Did you know?
Certain quails are migratory birds, while others spend most of their time on the ground and stay in the same area their entire lives.

R raced rabbit thinking it could win,
But rabbit left R whirling in a spin.
I gave her a root with a smiling face,
Then refreshed, she just tripled her pace.

My, oh my, it is so unclear.
Is this my perfect pet I hear?
Rabbits are rewarding, but how can I know?
There are so many letters with pets to show.

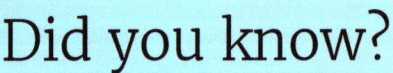

Did you know?

Rabbits have nearly 360° panoramic vision. They can see everything behind them and only have a small blind spot in front of their noses.

S suggested two swans, white as snow.
"I'm sure it's the best solution, you know.
Mating for life, they share a special bond,
Swimming, super silently, in the pond."

My, oh my, it is so unclear.
Is this my perfect pet I hear?
The swans are super sleek, but how can I know?
There are so many letters with pets to show.

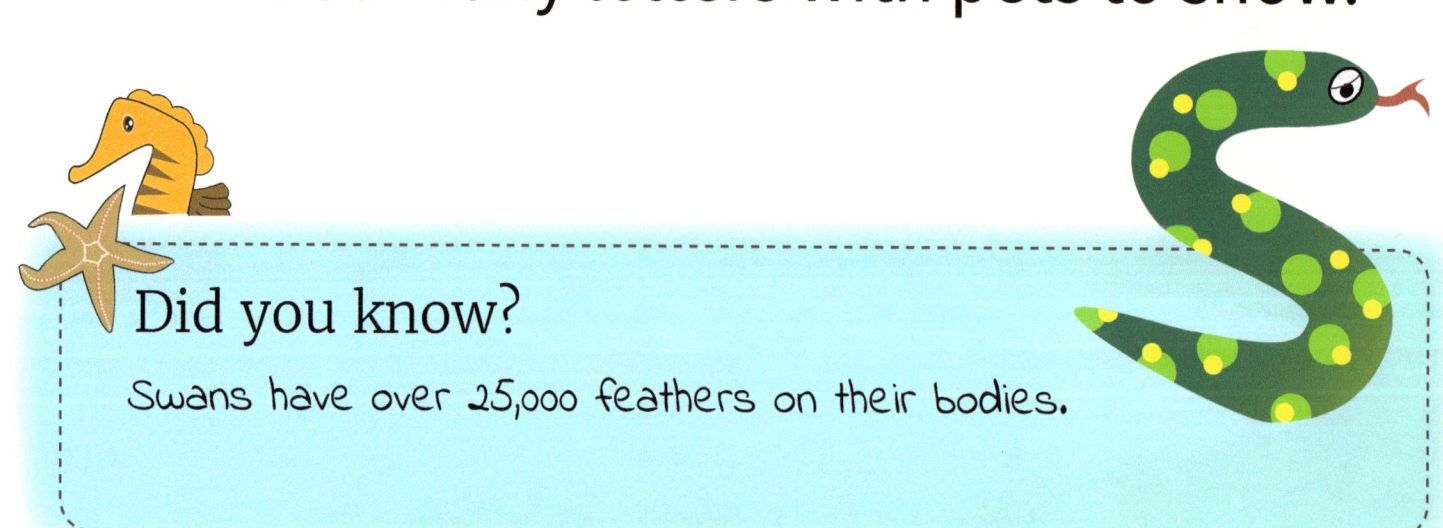

Did you know?
Swans have over 25,000 feathers on their bodies.

T took a tiny tiger, fun to hold.
"He will be tremendous, as I was told.
Master of the sneaky hunting technique,
Each striped cat is special and unique."

My, oh my, it is so unclear.
Is this my perfect pet I hear?
Tigers are terrific, but how can I know?
There are still more letters with pets to show.

Did you know?

The tiger is the biggest species of the cat family. There are more tigers held privately as pets than there are in the wild.

U urged me, "Get an umbrellabird!"
A real tropical bird, or so I've heard,
She lives in rainforests, where chicks are fed.
A large crest sits on the top of her head.

My, oh my, it is so unclear.
Is this my perfect pet I hear?
This rare bird is unique, but how can I know?
There are still more letters with pets to show.

Did you know?

The umbrellabird is a large, tropical species of bird that lives the rainforests of Central and South America.

V voted for a vulture, of all things.
He virtually glides on his wide wings.
His funny bald head is yellowish gold.
He tucks it in, whenever he feels cold.

My, oh my, it is so unclear.
Is this my perfect pet I hear?
A vulture is valuable, but how can I know?
There are still more letters with pets to show.

Did you know?

Vultures have wide, strong wings. They can glide in the air for hours looking down at the ground for a meal.

W wanted me to choose a wise wolf.
I like to listen to him howl and woof.
Living in the wilderness with a group,
To get his food, he joins a hunting troop.

My, oh my, it is so unclear.
Is this my perfect pet I hear?
A wolf is wonderful, but I still don't know.
There are a few more letters with pets to show.

Did you know?

Wolves develop strong social bonds. They demonstrate deep affection for their families and may even sacrifice themselves to protect the family unit.

X was excited with an x-ray fish,
An exotic pet anyone would wish.
His benefits are extra apparent.
His body is extremely transparent!

My, oh my, it is so unclear.
Is this my perfect pet I hear?
An x-ray fish excels, but I still don't know.
There are still two more letters with pets to show.

Did you know?

The translucent skin of the x-ray fish helps the fish blend in against rocks and plants, keeping him safe from being seen by predators.

Letter y yearned for a yellow baboon.
He really likes to take a nap at noon.
You will never see him on the highway,
But you can go find him in Zimbabwe.

My, oh my, it is so unclear.
Is this my perfect pet I hear?
I love them all, so I really do not know.
How can I choose one and let the others go?

Did you know?

Yellow baboons use over 30 vocalizations: grunts, barks and screams. Their non-vocal gestures include yawns, lip smacking, and shoulder shrugging.

Z zigzagged in with a zebra bright,
Shiny black with stripes brilliantly white.
"I have the perfect solution for you.
I will give you your own key to the zoo!"

Did you know?
Every zebra has a unique pattern of black and white stripes. In a herd of zebras, the stripes of all the zebras merge into a big mass making it hard for predators to single out individual animals to hunt.

About the book

I first started writing this book when I taught my own child, Yuli, the ABCs. I always believed that kids, especially at the younger ages, learn most efficiently when they are playing and having fun. I am also a strong believer that the learning process can be not only an educational experience but also a tool to strengthen the parent-child bond. With that in mind, I designed this book to develop phonological (sound) awareness through story, pictures, interactive activities for the child and adult reader to share.

Making the Most of the Book

As the story-poem progresses, each letter and the animal it presents are showcased in two stanzas that include words starting with the same letter as the animal. An accompanying illustration depicts the featured animal somewhere in the picture, often engaged in the activity described in the poem.

One interesting fact about each animal accompanies the illustration. These facts are just the tip of the iceberg of interesting information, and they are mainly meant to intrigue and encourage the child to find out more. You can encourage further learning by offering questions like where does this animal live? what does he like to eat? what helps him adapt to his habitat? For example: the story mentions that Kangaroo jumps high. You could ask the child, What helps kangaroos jump so high? The story also mentions kangaroos have a pouch to keep their babies in. You could suggest that you and the child look up what baby kangaroos are called (joeys). Questions could include, where do they live? Then upon learning that kangaroos live in central Australia, where it can be very hot and dry for weeks and where water is a precious commodity, you could ask what helps them survive in this habitat? One answer will often lead to another question. You and your child can find out the answers together from the Internet or other sources; you don't have to know everything.

Each illustration includes several other images of things, emotions, colors, actions, and numbers whose words start with the same featured letter. So, the picture becomes a game. Have fun with your child identifying the images that start with the relevant letter. Some words are very obvious and others are harder to find. You might even find yourself identifying new words after you have done this activity with your child a few times. It is always exciting to find a new word.

The words for each letter were chosen carefully to represent the basic, simple sounds that each letter makes, both the sound that says the letter's name and a variety of other short sounds it represents. More complex sounds that vowels make in combination with other letters, such as the o in owl, have been omitted so that the child can learn the vowel's phonetic (sound) range little by little. This will help your child develop phonological awareness, which is one of the bases of being able to read.

A note about X. In nearly all the words starting with X (except when X is a prefix in words like X-ray), the X makes a Z sound. This can be confusing to a young child, so this book doesn't include initial X words with Z sound. Later when your child is quite familiar with the book and the sounds it is introducing, you might talk about how X sometimes says "zzz" like Z and introduce xylophone and xeriscape.

The illustration is intended to be a launchpad to teach your child, foster curiosity, and introduce the child to research. For example, the illustrations can be a starting point for learning about the different places and cultures in the world. You might choose a country where the animal lives and together with your child locate it on the map, research the climate and culture of the country, and so on. You might also teach some science or astronomy starting with something in the illustration that corresponds to the letter. For example, V's illustration shows a volcano. You could explore volcanos with your child—how volcanos are formed, where volcanos are found, why some are dormant and other are active, and what happens when they erupt. This exploration could lead to other books or to the Internet. Similarly, each letter can be an introduction to one or more professions starting with the letter. This is an opportunity for a discussion about the importance of each profession, the training and skills needed, where the profession is performed, and value of work in general. Have any of the animals been characters in literature? If so, this book can lead to other books featuring the animal or any other topic that comes up and
interests the child.

Adding a bit of psychology and social understanding, violet Purely Critter, who is presented in each illustration, shows an emotion starting with the relevant letter (e.g., angry for A, happy for H.) You can name the critter with a name corresponding to the letter for that illustration and try to find answers for why he is feeling the way he does. Use as many relevant words for the letter as you can. For example, Leo is loathing that the lion is afraid of the lamb. (This is daughter Yuli's example.) Additional ideas for activities can be found in Miss Yuli's Class online at www.yulisclass.com.

Combining knowledge from different disciplines makes the learning more fun and interesting and promotes awareness of different fields of interest. It can also be helpful in identifying the child's interests, so that you can use those interests in presenting whatever other knowledge you want to share with the child.

We hope that you and the child you read with enjoy this book.

Merav Ben oved and the Development Team at Miss Yuli's Class.

Emotions

A	angry
B	blushed
C	crying
D	dirty
E	embarrassed
F	frown/frustrated
G	grateful
H	happy
I	inspired
J	joyful
K	kiss
L	love, laugh
M	mysterious

N	naughty
O	optimistic
P	proud
Q	quiet
R	relaxed
S	surprised
T	tired
U	upset
V	victorious
W	wink
X	excited
Y	yawn
Z	zip the mouth

www.ingramcontent.com/pod-product-compliance
Lightning Source LLC
Chambersburg PA
CBHW041533040426
42446CB00002B/67